LAPHAM'S
Rules of
INFLUENCE

LAPHAM'S
Rules of
INFLUENCE

A Careerist's Guide

to Success, Status, and

Self-Congratulation

LEWIS LAPHAM

RANDOM HOUSE   NEW YORK

Library of Congress Cataloging-in-Publication Data

Lapham, Lewis H.
Lapham's rules of influence: a careerist's guide to success,
status, and self-congratulation / Lewis Lapham.—1st ed.
p.   cm.
ISBN 0-679-42605-1 (alk. paper)
1. Rich people—United States.   2. Rich people—Social
life and customs.   3. Successful people—United States.
4. Life skills.   5. United States—Social life and customs.
I. Title
HC110.W4L2398   1999
332.024—dc21   98-33212

Random House website address: www.atrandom.com

Printed in the United States of America on acid-free paper

2   4   6   8   9   7   5   3

First Edition

BOOK DESIGN BY BARBARA M. BACHMAN

FOR DELPHINA LAPHAM,

WHO NEVER LEARNED

ANY OF THE RULES

INTRODUCTION

INTRODUCTION

AMBITION HATH NO MEAN,
IT IS EITHER UPON ALL FOURS
OR UPON TIPTOES.

•

—*George Savile, Marquis of Halifax*

AS THE EDITOR OF A MAGAZINE WITH OFFICES IN NEW YORK, I talk to a good many young people newly arrived in the city with the hope of finding a career—if not in the literary trades, then somewhere in Wall Street or television—and over the last ten or fifteen years I have listened to their questions turn thin and cold. A generation ago the graduates of the country's well-to-do universities might have mentioned the name of a dead poet, or said something about truth and its untimely betrayals. Not now. Not when they think that if they miss their first and maybe only chance at the brass ring, they might never find their way back to the putting greens of Fairfield County or the music on the beach at Malibu.

The philosophical questions have gone missing in action, rendered futile by the prices paid for New York apartments, and although I sometimes come across a wandering idealist intent upon saving an orphan or a whale, mostly I meet people to whom the fervors of social protest seem superfluous or quaint. They don't talk about changing the system, only about the means of improving their access to it, and they smile with their mouths but not their eyes. Impatient with metaphors and bored by sentiment, eager to advance the token of their lives around the Monopoly board of the standard American success, they present themselves as candidates for a life of privilege and ease. Instead of wondering how to catch a falling star or who cleft the devil's foot, they ask for introductions to Woody Allen and the doorman at Balthazar, about the hope of meeting Peter Jennings and the name of the restaurant where the editors of the Condé Nast magazines go expensively to lunch.

I wish I thought their questions misplaced, but even the dullest students of the American economic scene haven't failed to notice the widening chasm between rich and poor, or the increasingly obvious disparities between the civic-minded theory taught in school and the profit-making facts posted on the walls of the news and entertainment media. As was true in the early years of the American republic, the country is governed by a commercial oligarchy, but the oligarchy has become so all-encompassing, and the broad mass of the American people so dependent upon its corporate whim—for work, pension, medical care, club membership, views of Europe—that the business of getting ahead in the world comes to resemble what the eighteenth century would have recognized as the art of "obtaining a place at court."

The art is one at which Americans have long been skilled. George Washington at the age of sixteen copied out 110 *Rules of Civility and Decent Behavior in Company and Conversation* (e.g., "shift not your self in sight of others, nor gnaw your nails"; "Do not puff up the cheeks; loll not out the tongue . . ."), and Benjamin Franklin in eighteenth-century Philadelphia improved the readers of his *Poor Richard's Almanack* with adages intended to teach the mechanics of self-advancement. Favoring the persona of "the humble inquirer," Franklin didn't neglect to mention the virtues of honor, industry, and thrift, but neither did he fail to recommend prudence, caution, and coldness of heart—e.g., "the weakest foe boasts some revenging Pow'r; the weakest friend some serviceable hour."

A worldy philosopher and a friend to Mammon, Franklin was the most popular author in colonial America, his books and pamphlets more eagerly sought and sooner read than the sermons descended from the pulpits of Protestant conscience. The preachers followed the line of Cotton Mather, who had counseled his seventeenth-century congregations in Massachusetts to distinguish between true success, which was spiritual, and the mere getting of riches, which was material and therefore imperfect. Not that Mather didn't expect the faithful to be up and doing and making as much money as possible, but one did so in order to glorify God, to provide the means of doing good for others as well as for oneself. If Franklin thought it "hard for an empty bag to stand upright," Mather thought it "unrighteous" for a full bag to rest content on the weight of its tea or gold, and for the first 200 years of the American journey the guides pointing the way to the kingdom of heaven often fell to quarreling about who among them was looking at the right map.

THE EVENTS OF THE nineteenth century conspired against the Puritan contempt for place-seeking popinjays (the sort of people whom Mather associated with the corruption at the court of Charles II), and when Alexis de Tocqueville passed through Nashville in the winter of 1831, he remarked on the unexpected liveliness of what he called "the courtier spirit" in the United States. He had thought that the citizens of the new democracy would prove to be turbulent and rough-hewn people, direct in their actions and forthright in their speech. He was surprised to find them so adept in the uses of servility. True, they didn't dress as well as the ladies and gentlemen in France; their conversation wasn't as refined, and neither were their manners, but they possessed a native talent for ingratiating themselves with anyone who could do them a service or grant them a privilege. The effect was often comic—dandies in broadcloth instead of silk brocade, loud in their brag and fantastic in their gestures—but the intention was as earnest as it was humorless.

After considering the paradox for some years, Tocqueville concluded that in a monarchy the courtier spirit was less pervasive than it was in a democracy. Under the rule of a monarch the courtier spirit crowds in upon the palace, and even the most arrogant of kings seldom could muster the gall to speak in the name of any interest other than his own. A democracy claims to serve the interest of the sovereign people, and because the figure of the prince wears so many faces (network executive, syndicated columnist, congressman, corporate CEO, town clerk) the relatively few favors in a monarch's gift (sinecure, benefice, patents royal) become the cornucopia of grace and favor distributed under the nominally egalitarian rubrics of tax exemption, defense contract, publication, milk subsidy, tenure. The courtier spirit seeps through the whole of the society, and the expectant capitalist is constantly bowing and smiling in eight or nine different directions, forever turning, like a compass needle or a weather vane, into the wind of the new money. When everything is more or less the same, and when everybody can compete on the same footing for the same inventories of reward, the slightest variation of result produces a sickness of heart, which, as Tocqueville observed, places the courtier spirit "within easy reach of the multitude," because so many people have so much to gain by prostituting themselves to the mob, to the newspapers, to the wisdom of the rich. The more equal people become, the more urgent their desire for inequality and the more feverish their buying in the markets of self-esteem.

Toward the end of the nineteenth century, in the heyday of the Gilded Age, Horatio Alger sketched the portrait of the triumphant young American in a series of popular books about street urchins supposedly rising from rags to riches by dint of their hard work and noble character. Closer examination of the texts shows them to be lessons in the school of flattery. The Tattered Toms and Ragged Dicks succeed as perfect sycophants who happen to be standing in the right place at the right time, encountering by accident a benign plutocrat for whom they play the part of dutiful and obliging son and so inherit the fortune. Alger's heroes were made to the measure of the times, consistent with P. T. Barnum's contention that "money-getters are the benefactors of our race," and John D. Rockefeller's silencing the objections of a grumbling clergyman with the statement "Money printed your Bible."

The twentieth century replaced what was left of the emphasis on inward grace (wealth the product of virtue) with an emphasis on outward favor (wealth the product of personality), and the bestselling guides to big-time success (Dale Carnegie's *How to Win Friends and Influence People*, Norman Vincent Peale's *The Power of Positive Thinking*) applied the techniques of the advertising business to the problems of personal image management. More in the spirit of Franklin than Mather, the vast bulk of our own popular literature, books as well as the self-help manuals, the fashion magazines, and the Wall Street tip sheets, now largely consists of instructions meant to set the attentive reader on the right road to Hilton Head or Palm Beach. Do what you're told, follow the directions on the label, and you too will enter paradise on the American Express gold card.

Against the great and swelling hymn to conformity, our college commencement speakers sometimes bring forth the familiar image of the American patriot imbued with the spirit of dissent. They present the American hero as the voice of conscience, forever crying in the wilderness, standing on a principled soapbox to announce an eternal and unwelcome truth. Although we like to weave the story of our fabled individualism from the thread of frontier cloth (gaunt, stiff-necked figures, solitary and self-reliant, forever striding west), when given the chance to wander into the mountains or follow the call of the wild, we fall back behind the lines of our prepared excuses and check into the nearest cage. As Tocqueville understood in the forests of Tennessee, Americans don't have much use for their well-advertised freedom of speech. He found them cowed by what he called "the tyranny of the majority," and it occurred to him that never in his travels had he encountered a people so fearful of free expression as the supposedly boisterous Americans. Too many of them were too afraid of losing a fraction of advantage or a degree of self-importance, and so they were very, very careful about talking out of turn.

Maybe I've lived too long in New York City, or attended too many journalism seminars, but Tocqueville's observation strikes me as neither strange nor remote. I don't know to what extent the courtier spirit flourished in the years between 1831 and 1980, but certainly over the span of the last twenty years it has grown sleek and fat, and within the framework of my own experience and fairly wide acquaintance very seldom does anybody say or do anything that might harm his or her chance of preferment. When I think of the American elite assembled in some conference center or hotel ballroom, I see a great throng of eager and anxious faces—too many to count or to name, nearly all of them willing to do or say whatever is required in return for a camera angle or a contribution to the alumni fund, for a page of advertising, a letter of credit, a word of praise. Applauding the divine wisdom of whoever happens to be buying the golf balls or the salmon on toast, the well-dressed company chatters about who is in and who is out, who will come and who will go, and the image that usually comes to mind is that of a crowd of flatterers managing their ambitions as deftly as the ladies and gentlemen of the king's bedchamber in Louis XIV's palace at Versailles.

Approached by means of a database instead of by anecdote, the broad outline of American court society might be plotted on a graph that takes into account the boards of directors of the Fortune 500 as well as the trustees of the nation's leading universities, the senior staffs of the major news media, the partners of the larger law firms, the principal figures of the movie business, and the custodians of the prominent policy institutes and philanthropic foundations; the resulting database would encompass the few hundred thousand people who own and operate the country and govern the shaping of the American mind—who manage the government, control the media and the banks, write the academic curricula and the television commercials. Among their surprisingly anxious and beleaguered company, the rights of purchase serve as proofs of salvation, and most of the individuals who enjoy most of the country's advantages divide into two categories of nervous spendthrift—the parvenu rich rising to the surface of their ambition, the ci-devant rich sinking into the depths of anonymity. Neither order ever seems to have enough money to sustain what it deems to be an appropriate measure of comfort and respect, and I don't think I've met more than thirty or forty of their number who could be fairly described (by themselves or anybody else) as democrats; they would think the noun too common. Preferring to regard themselves as members of a privileged class, as holders of various entitlements or keepers of the nation's conscience, they fix the value of their self-worth by their association or acquaintance with expensive labels—names of exclusive clubs and well-defended suburbs, names of polo shirts and media syndicates, of hotel concierges, Hollywood restaurants and celebrities.

DURING THE EARLY YEARS of the American republic almost everyone was self-employed, and the citizen whom Jefferson or Madison had in mind was somebody free to tell any other citizen precisely what he thought of his lying contract or his filthy shop. As late as the first decade of the twentieth century, roughly 90 percent of the American people were still self-employed, for the most part living on small family farms; by 1998 their number had dwindled to 4 percent. The United States in the meantime had so arranged its financial affairs that 10 percent of the population held at least 70 percent of the nation's wealth, and 5 percent of the population owned all of the nation's capital assets. If by 1998 it was no longer possible to pretend that everybody was as equal as everybody else, it was equally clear that the sustained prosperity of the last decades of the twentieth century had brought into being the

American equivalent of a *rentier* class, and as the balance of the society's wealth has become more heavily weighted in favor of a more narrowly circumscribed oligarchy, the arts of deference here become more refined. Whether dressed up as executives or bellhops, the employees depend upon their corporate or institutional overlord, not only for wages but also for the definitions of self, and the man who cannot make his own estate must accommodate himself to the increasingly exquisite appetites of his patrons. If political freedom is conditional upon economic freedom, then the citizen who cannot afford to voice an opinion contrary to the opinion of the executive editor or the director of sales forfeits an owner's interest in his or her own mind, and learns, of necessity, to dance the beggar's waltz.

Large tracts of the country undoubtedly remain uncontaminated by the stale air of complacent privilege, and no day passes without fresh reports of new fortunes in Silicon Valley, new openings to the Internet, new discoveries in the sciences, America possessed of so many genies in the bottles of invention that even the government's swarm of zealous clerks cannot keep track of all the people experimenting with the properties of hydrogen, merging computer companies, deciphering the genetic codes. Major-league coaches don't align the batting order or the defensive backfield with the whim of the owner's mistress, and I'm sure that within numerous other industries and professions (even within some college English departments) a great many individuals achieve their places in the world primarily by means of their talent, their intelligence, and their character. But I've met so few of them over the last twenty-odd years that I incline to think of them as anomalies, people who have accomplished their purpose against increasingly heavy odds.

What else is the courtier spirit if not the spirit of a society guided by talk-show hosts, captained by lawyers, inspired by actors, educated by press agents—all of them the kind of people paid to arrange the truth in its most flattering and convenient poses? How else to define the courtier spirit if not as the languages of political correctness taught in southern churches and northern universities? We spend our days filling out forms, begging the stamps of official approval and permission, currying the favor of a foundation grant, an academic appointment, a government contract, counting it our duty to strike attractive poses, to pass vaguely through a room while displaying the finery of our moral sentiments, finding our way in the world by saying to a succession of masters, "Make of me what you want; I am what you want me to be." Read through the roster of ornamental American names of whom one thinks when composing a guest list or choosing a college president, and the common traits of character and mind suggest "the plastic capability" that President Nixon so much admired in General Alexander Haig and that Senator Robert Dole adopted to the purposes of the 1996 presidential campaign when he said to a crowd of Republicans in Orange County, California, "If you want me to be Ronald Reagan, I'll be Ronald Reagan."

Although I cannot measure the courtier spirit as would a tailor—by seam or collar point or sleeve length—I can see it in a gesture or hear it in a turn of phrase. Henry Kissinger struck the preferred tone of devout sycophancy in the summer of 1971, when he attached a handwritten note to the advance text of what he knew to be another one of Richard Nixon's dissembling speeches about Vietnam—"No matter what the result, free people everywhere will be forever in your debt, your serenity during crises, your steadfastness under pressure, have been all that prevented the triumph of mass hysteria. It has been an inspiration to serve. As always, H." Barbara Walters struck the proper note of subservience when in the course of interviewing a newly elected Jimmy Carter in the autumn of 1976, she said, in a breathless and scarcely audible murmur, "Be kind to us, Mr. President. Be good to us." President Bush hit upon the appropriate tone of insolence during the 1988 election campaign when he refused to answer a rude question about an American naval blunder in the Persian Gulf (the shooting down of an Iranian airliner and the abrupt murder of its 242 passengers) on the ground that he would "never, never apologize for the United States of America . . . I don't care what the facts are."

Like President Reagan before him, Bush presented himself to the American people in the character of the perfect courtier, possessed of a résumé that he once described, as proudly as a boy with a stamp collection, as "all these fantastic credentials," his rise to power dependent upon the gift of patronage, the story of his life the story of making polite small talk (about the weather in Maine or the chance of nuclear war), always remembering to write little notes of sympathy or praise, glad to revise or discard any thought deemed unsuitable to the occasion, passing the drinks and the watercress sandwiches, laughing at all the rich men's jokes.

President Clinton has proved himself equally accommodating, another man for all seasons content to promote the ritual fictions of a sham democracy. Accepting the Democratic presidential nomination at Madison Square Garden in New York in the summer of 1992, Clinton did his best to show himself as a candidate who shunned the word *liberal*, proud to declare his faith in "entrepreneurial government" and "the noble endeavor of American business," careful to avoid any close association with those factions of the Democratic party (intellectuals, Blacks, the poor) likely to remind people that he was not a Republican. He adjusted his promises to reflect the findings of a poll or a focus group, and over the course of the campaign he described himself as "pro business and pro labor," "for economic growth and for protecting the environment," "for affirmative action but against quotas," "for legal abortions but also for making abortion as rare as possible."

Once elected to the White House and so obliged to reward his patrons and comfort his fans, Clinton provided the former with the gifts of office and the latter with a $17 million inaugural pageant. While the Congress on Capitol Hill went about the business of confirming the president's nominees to the Cabinet, most of them corporate lawyers, several of them patently unqualified or inept, all of them loyal servants of the status quo that candidate Clinton had so often decried as timid, self-serving, and corrupt, President Clinton appeared as the friend of the common man in a series of *tableaux vivants* staged against the backdrops of Washington's best-known monuments. Bill Clinton at

Monticello departing for the Capitol under the aegis of Thomas Jefferson; Bill Clinton by candlelight, approaching the Lincoln Memorial on foot; Bill Clinton ringing a replica of the Liberty Bell; Bill Clinton listening, transfixed, to Diana Ross sing "We Are the World" and to ten saxophonists playing Elvis Presley's "Heartbreak Hotel"; Bill Clinton in tears at the Capitol Center, accepting the badges and emblems of democratic sentiment at the hands of Barbra Streisand and Michael Jackson; Bill Clinton swearing the oath of office in the presence of Maya Angelou, who read an ode to the multicultural composition (". . . the Asian, the Hispanic, the Jew/ The African, the Native American, the Sioux. . . . The Gay, the Straight, the Preacher/ The privileged, the homeless, the Teacher . . .") of the American soul.

Marked from its inception by the quality of weightlessness and comfortably adapted to the floating realm of images that constitutes the kingdom of celebrity, the modus operandi of the Clinton administration presupposes a world in which words stand surrogate for deeds, and truth is a stage prop, like the palm fronds and the handsome chairs.

By the time Clinton stood for his second term in the prosperous autumn of 1996, the voters were well enough acquainted with his character to know him as a man ruled by expedience, probably a philanderer, certainly a liar. But he put up a good show, forever bowing and smiling into the glare of the new money. Brilliant in the performance of his ceremonial duties— handing out ballpoint pens in the White House Rose Garden, dismissing a surgeon general for her mention of the word "masturbation," apologizing for slavery, exhorting the nation's teenage youth to take a vow of chastity—somehow he never quite managed to cast the airiness of his rhetoric in anything other than a courtier's gracious but empty phrase.

ALTHOUGH THE MOST ELABORATE of the nation's courts resides in Washington, the country is large enough and rich enough to sustain a multitude of lesser thrones and dominions. Courts form like oyster shells not only around the pearls of great price at IBM and the Walt Disney Company but also around Oprah Winfrey and Greg Norman. Citibank commands the fealty of more people than lived in Elizabethan London; George Steinbrenner holds in his gift a larger sum of patronage than was available to Cosimo de Medici, and Robert Redford entertains requests for campaign money only from those political candidates who have sworn their allegiance to trees. Most of the correspondents who have had occasion to describe the life at court—among them Shakespeare, La Bruyère, Saint-Simon, Jonathan Swift, our own long list of once-upon-a-time Hollywood insiders or White House aides-de-camp— remark on the atmospheres of suffocating malevolence. Nobody fails to admire the magnificence of the marble pillars or the wonders of the electronic equipment, but neither does anybody fail to mention, as did Benjamin Franklin at the court of George III, "numberless and needless places, enormous salaries, pensions, perquisites, bribes, groundless quarrels, foolish expeditions, false accounts or no accounts, contracts and jobs that devour all revenue . . ."

Because the careerist so obviously and so precariously hangs from the trapeze of his connections, the poor wretch can never escape the feeling of weightlessness and dread. If everything is made of appearances, of images and gestures instead of blood or stone or thought, then everything can disappear at a moment's notice. The guests at court—aka "we happy few"—drift through their schedules in an all but constant state of panic. To the extent that the meaning of their existence becomes synonymous with the striking of poses that could be as easily sustained by Red Grooms or Zsa Zsa Gabor, they know themselves to be superfluous, which is why the courtier spirit is about the wish to make time stand still, about being, not becoming. The possibility of change, in the arts and sciences as well as in the political or commercial orders, does too much damage to the resident self-esteem. God forbid that the world might be transformed by some unknown physicist or anonymous computer program, or by an obscure despot at work somewhere on an island with a name that nobody can pronounce. The acute states of anxiety give rise to the urgent need for reassurance, and anybody who would be somebody thus spends his days accumulating badges and credentials, publishing unintelligible treatises in the journals that enjoy the favor of the court (*Foreign Affairs*, the *Wilson Quarterly*, the *Harvard Business Review*), joining the proper clubs (Cosmos, Century, Duquesne, Pacific Union), worrying about the very best and most significant questions of the day (the environmental catastrophe, the new world order, nuclear weapons escaped from the arsenal of the old Soviet Union), decorating each other with awards and prizes, traveling to conferences in Colorado or Switzerland for no other reason than that they should be noticed. It doesn't matter what the courtier has to say (assuming, of course, that he says nothing offensive or impolite), and it doesn't matter whether he contributes by his going to London or Geneva even the slightest mote of useful service. The important thing is to be seen at the fetes of the prince—whether in Texas for the quail shooting, on a golf course with Michael Jordan, or writing for *The New York Review of Books.*

Not that the court is averse to merit or talent. Nothing so pleases the ambitious courtier as the chance to fawn upon a statesman whom he can mistake for Metternich or a novelist whom he can confuse with Tolstoy, but if he cannot tell the difference between Metternich and Madeleine Albright, or between Tolstoy and Philip Roth, he must content himself with the effigies endorsed by the smiling favor of the gossip columns. It is quite possible that somebody might write a good book and even be congratulated for doing so by *The New York Times;* it is equally possible that the Ford Foundation will award a research grant to a scientist capable of useful and original work. Such things sometimes happen. They fall within the category of happy accident, and they justify, at least for the time being and much to everybody's satisfaction and relief, the pretensions of the institution awarding the titles and degrees. Once instructed in the correct forms of agreeable behavior and expedient speech, the talented careerist in attendance at one court finds it a simple matter to perform the same services for other well-placed patrons in other well-lighted rooms, to move from the White House press office to the studios of ABC News, from the glory of Edgar Bronfman to the splendor of Warren Beatty. If it is possible to lick one boot, then, with a little patience and not very much practice, it is possible to lick the boots of a regiment.

But before moving forward to the parade ground of a five-star American success, the candidates for a life of ease and privilege must first discard negative stereotypes and false impressions. The exercise isn't as hard as it might seem. Mostly it is a matter of what college English departments describe as a labor of deconstruction and one with which I've had some experience over the years, because the new graduates of Harvard or the University of Michigan who arrive in New York with résumés as carefully groomed as the dachshunds at the Westminster Dog Show also bring with them the old literary vocabularies of Puritan suspicion and contempt. "Connections" they understand, and "networking" they appreciate in its usages as both verb and noun, but they flinch at the words "toady," "brown-nose," "sycophant," "lickspittle," "flunky," "parasite," "hanger-on," "suck-up," "leech." All good homespun words, as near to the heart of an American success as E-Z credit and no money down, but too often employed as insults instead of compliments. Apparently unaware that the best of their countrymen's novels, most notably those of Henry James, Edith Wharton, and F. Scott Fitzgerald, talk about the establishing of one's position in society, the would-be little friends of all the world tend to think of the courtier's art as somehow un-American, to associate it with a costume drama they once saw on the History Chanel or PBS. Nor does it occur to them that the making of one's way across a parquet floor now presents far fewer difficulties than it did in the Gilded Age. Had they been born into the world of Wharton or James they might have been expected to dress for dinner, to display an acquaintance with classical literature, to play the piano or speak Italian. The Edwardian aspirations to cultural grandeur went down with the

Titanic, and contemporary American society requires of its aspirants nothing more than the capacity to add and subtract. Know the magnitude of the money standing in the room and make one's bows accordingly. The numbers stand surrogate for further efforts of imaginative definition; the larger the number, the more magnificent the personality, the more necessary the corporation, the more beautiful the dress. An actress occupying a $2 million beach house outranks an actress quartered in a $1 million bungalow. A financier possessed of $4 billion deserves a deeper show of respect than the art dealer possessed of a mere $1 billion. Transfer the simple calculation to the whole canvas of American society, and the portrait is as easy to understand as a Renaissance painting in which the richest of the artist's patrons kneel closest to the newborn or the dying Christ.

A few of the more seriously misinformed students sometimes cast the nets of their scorn over careerists as admirable as Henry Kissinger and Oliver North, even over panderers as accomplished as Colin Powell and Barbara Walters. Their faculty-lounge sarcasms follow from a misreading of American history as well as of the daily newspapers, and more often than not the confusions can be corrected by a short series of questions and answers arranged in the form of what passes in the commercial city of New York as postmodern Socratic dialogue:

Q: What constitutes an American success?

A: Money in the bank, a house in the country, one's name in the columns.

Q: What else?

A: The deference of department-store clerks, a place at the table in one of the country's better corporate boardrooms, invitations to the White House and the Academy Awards ceremony, the homage of headwaiters, a Pulitzer Prize.

Q: Why then rail against the people who possess in large abundance the objects of your own desire?

A: They achieve them by dubious means.

Q: But what means are dubious in a society that raises selfishness to the power of supreme virtue—good for business, good for the stock market, good for America?

A: Some means are better than others.

Q: To whom do the distinctions matter? To the president of the United States?

A: The president is made of wax.

Q: To ABC News?

A: The media grovel for ratings.

Q: To the members of Congress or the deans of universities?

A: Members of Congress and deans of universities spend 80 percent of their time bobbing for the coins of subsidy.

Q: Why then refuse to play by the house rules? Why decline the invitation to the beggar's waltz?

A: I am a person of moral quality.

Q: But who will thank you for your fine phrases and stalwart principles?

A: The editors of *The New York Review of Books*.

Q: If you're not in, you're out, and when was out a better place to be?

A: Long ago and far away and sometimes in the poems of William Butler Yeats.

The conversations don't always proceed along precisely the same lines—sometimes they raise a question about whether it is more fun to drink bad wine in Cuernavaca than to ride in triumph through the streets of Santa Monica (it isn't), or whether the proofs of honor can be exchanged for travel miles (they can't)—but it usually doesn't need much more than an hour for the humble inquirers to understand that when presented with Molière's *Tartuffe* or Seymour Hersh's portrait of John F. Kennedy, they should read the text as a cheerful self-help manual, not as bitter social satire.

An hour is time enough to make the general observation about the wrongheadedness of so many of our latter-day newspaper sermons regretting America's fall from its imaginary state of innocence and grace, but the most humble of the humble inquirers seek further explanations and supplementary rules of conduct. Impressed by their zeal but not always able to address their concerns about the finer points of etiquette, I've made notes over the last few years of their most frequently asked questions. The notes take the form of simple precepts and helpful suggestions, and although the indicated lines of approach don't guarantee a safe arrival on the sunny heights of an American success, at least they encourage a correct posture and a proper tone. The list is by no means complete (nothing about cosmetic surgery, no mention of horses), but I like to think that any additional questions—about a first husband's funeral, the importance of pheasants, an outbreak of war or semiotics—can be answered by glancing at the jewelry of the other people in the room.

—December 1998, New York

MORNING

APPEARANCES

---

*T*heir rule is sovereign, and you quarrel with them at your peril. Seeing is believing, and you are the sum of what you seem.

In Philadelphia in 1743 the immortal Benjamin Franklin, still a young printer but wise beyond his years, took the trouble to be seen on Market Street every day at noon, pushing a wheelbarrow stacked with reams of blank paper—not because the paper needed to go anywhere, but because Franklin was promoting his reputation for diligence, industry, and thrift.

The times have changed but not the principle, which is why you always rent the Ferrari when visiting Los Angeles or run up a $500 phone bill when staying for three days in a New York hotel—to promote the impression that you are very busy, never out of touch with Rupert Murdoch or Michael Eisner.

Some of the country's conservative churches and liberal universities make invidious comparisons between appearances and what they call reality. The distinction is malicious and false, a cruel punishment visited upon thirteen generations of otherwise happy Americans by Puritan clergymen who objected to the display of gold lace.

FIRST IMPRESSIONS

---

*T*he first impression is also the last impression, which is why it is important to always wear clean shoes. You don't wish to be remembered as the stain on the rug.

CHOOSING COMPANIONS

*S*eek out the acquaintance of people richer and
more important than yourself and never take an
interest in people who cannot do you any favors.
This rule admits of no exceptions. When Henry
Kissinger was secretary of state, he put it plainly
to a woman seated next to him at a Washington
dinner party. "A great nation," he said, "is like an
ambitious hostess. It cannot afford to invite
unsuccessful people to its parties."

In the event that you become either rich
or famous you may collect friends in the way that
Nike acquires prize athletes or Philip II of Spain
collected dwarfs.

O PTIMISM

———————

Your fellow countrymen like upbeat, happy
people, and if you come up against bad news—
a missing child, the loss of your right hand, your
name left off the guest list for Barbra Streisand's
birthday party—imitate the television anchorpersons,
who manage to smile brightly when reading the
reports of floods in Ohio or massacre in Rwanda.
Never forget that you are always having fun. The
attitude is especially important when being
arraigned on charges of sodomy or tax evasion.

THE RÉSUMÉ

The most important of the American literary forms. Aspire to the magnificence of Richard Darman, a Washington careerist of the first rank who moved from the White House staff to the Treasury Department in the autumn of 1985 and took with him a letter of praise that he had himself composed for President Reagan's signature, a letter that awarded to its author all the credit for all the great works of Reagan's first term in office.

"Your abilities, your intelligence, and your willingness to work long hours are well known in Washington because they have been your trademark for many years. With such an extraordinary combination of talents, there is no question in my mind that you could have been a success in any career you chose. But, while you have been successful in both the business and academic worlds, you have chosen to devote yourself instead to a career that has chiefly been oriented toward public service. Knowing you as I do, I know it is your deep love of America, and your strong belief in its future greatness, that has impelled you to make this choice."

Commit the letter to memory. It speaks with the voice of genius.

ON BEING NICE

---

*T*he percentages favor the practice. You never know who might show up in a position to do you a good turn, to perform, in Benjamin Franklin's phrase, "some serviceable hour."

Two days before President Nixon left the White House in disgrace, Katherine Graham, the publisher of *The Washington Post,* sent him a courteous note, wishing him Godspeed and looking forward to a happier time when they might get together for cocktails. Mrs. Graham's paper had done the president a good deal of harm: it had discovered the news of the Watergate burglary, relentlessly pursued the story for two years through the long series of congressional investigations, tirelessly advanced the cause of Mr. Nixon's impeachment. And yet here was Mrs. Graham, a principal figure in what the president regarded as the liberal media conspiracy responsible for his ruin, writing a little note of sentimental farewell. She understood that the departing president might once again be transformed into a wise statesman, a marketable commodity, or a god.

WORDS

---

*E*xcept when filling out insurance claims or marking up the pages of a mail-order catalogue, give more thought to the adjectives than to the nouns. Words serve as set decorations. What matters is how they look and sound, not whatever it is that they supposedly mean.

The abstract word is always to be preferred to the concrete word, and the best of all possible words— "postmodern," "amusing," "enigmatic," "global," "empowering"—are those that can be addressed to both a foreign policy and the soup.

Proper usage depends upon prior recognition of the consensus already seated on the terrace or the lawn. In conservative company—at a yacht club in Orange County, California, say, or at a fund-raising dinner sponsored by the friends of Senator Orrin Hatch—the words, "sexist" and "racist" refer to people like Jesse Jackson or Woody Allen. Among avowed liberals gathered on West Seventy-ninth Street in Manhattan to celebrate a new book of essays by Gloria Steinem, the same two words describe the entire male populations of West Virginia, Arizona, and Tennessee.

THE NORM OF
MEDIOCRITY

A show of superior knowledge, per-
ception, or taste usually is as self-defeating as being
seen to think on television.

Conceal the marks of intelligence as if they were
warts or running sores, and take to heart the advice of
the late Paul D. Cravath, patriarch of the New York
law firm of Cravath, Swaine & Moore, who was speaking to a quorum of young and ambitious lawyers: "Brilliant intellectual powers are not essential; too much
imagination, too much wit, too great cleverness, too
facile fluency, if not leavened by a sound sense of pro-
portion, are quite as likely to impede success as to promote it. The best clients are apt to be afraid of those
qualities."

If the world arranged itself along the lines set forth by men and women of genius, how would it be possible to elect a president or bestow an Academy Award? Who could anybody invite to dinner?

READINESS

---

*P*icture an acrobat waiting for a trapeze,
and hold yourself in the same state of readiness.
You never know when you might be asked to
London for a conference, to Aspen for the skiing,
to the men's room for an enema or a line of cocaine.

THE BEGGAR'S WALTZ

---

*R*ich people must be approached with the same care that one brings to the stalking of a wildebeest or an elk. Their money is their life, and you are asking them for blood. Bear in mind George Washington's thirty-seventh rule of *Civility and Decent Behavior in Company and Conversation*—"In speaking to men of quality do not lean nor look them full in the face, nor approach too near them. At least keep a full pace from them."

Imagine yourself in a dance class and run through the repertoire of graceful positions—attentive, fawning, doe-eyed, steadfast, humble, struck dumb with awe. Arrange papers, open doors, push forward chairs. Only in the presence of important gossip columnists is it necessary to crawl.

The courting of would-be patrons with new money implies the sound of a different music than the courting of would-be patrons with old money. New money is more sprightly, more up tempo, more impressed by dramatic leaps. Think of John Travolta in *Saturday Night Fever*. Old money admires the slower movements of a minuet. Think of movies made from Jane Austen's novels or Shakespeare's plays.

CLICHÉS

*M*ake unsparing use of them.
The empty word is the correct word. Contrary
to the opinion of snobbish New York intellectuals,
the placid murmur of cliché is always preferable to
sharp insight or strong feeling. Think of waterfalls
in the lobbies of Hyatt hotels. Practice the sound
by reading aloud the essays of Roger Rosenblatt
or the editorial page of *The Washington Post*.

DRESS

---

*A*ny doubts on the questions of costume should be resolved in favor of unobtrusive colors and inconspicuous ornament. Celebrities of large magnitude can afford to make fashion statements, to express what their publicists call their "personality." Careerists not yet granted the privilege of a licensed self should seek to inspire confidence and respect, to convey the impression that their clothes, like their opinions, match the furniture and the drapes. Uniforms are always good, a tuxedo never a mistake.

CURIOSITY

---

*N*ever be seen to be taking notes or asking more than a few polite questions to which you don't expect important answers. Too much curiosity is a mark of inferior rank. You will be mistaken for a tourist or a waiter.

BADGES AND
CREDENTIALS

---

*A*ccumulate as many as possible. They serve
the same purpose as military campaign ribbons, and
one of these days somebody will figure out a way to
wear them on a yachting blazer or an evening dress.
If in public you proclaim your belief in the great
American idea that all men are created equal, in
private you must do what needs to be done to prove
yourself unequal. Large collections of exclusive
memberships and honorary degrees make the
weight of a British title.

MEETINGS

A good meeting is one at which nothing happens. The work has already been done by the staff, and the participants read from scripts like those given to the shepherds in a nursery-school Christmas pageant. Sit erect, second all the motions, remember everybody's name.

The last point cannot be too heavily stressed. Most people hear in the music of their own names the sweetest sound in the English language. Don't mispronounce it; repeat it as often as possible.

E U P H E M I S M

———————

*T*o speak too plainly is invariably a mistake, especially on matters likely to wound the vanity of the patron on whom you depend for your parking privileges. Study the advertisements for cosmetics and detergents, and learn to speak a language that is salt-free, risk-averse, baby-soft.

Conceive of yourself as a room-freshener and remember always the exemplary communiqué from General William Westmoreland, commander of American forces during the regrettable war in Vietnam, who said of the little Vietnamese girl blazing with the light of napalm, that he had been told, and so believed, that she was burned by an hibachi grill.

PRIVATE PLANES

---

*N*ever miss the chance to travel on a private plane. You're likely to meet somebody important, and if the plane happens to be going to Minneapolis or Palm Beach when you had been meaning to go to San Francisco or Boston, the gain of access makes good the loss of convenience.

Don't bring drugs (the plane could be confiscated) and wear old clothes (they express your appreciation of a private plane as a necessity, not a luxury). If the owner is not present do not attempt to hire his mistress or his golf caddie. Refrain from asking the pilot to buzz Yosemite.

STEPPING STONES

———

*B*ess Myerson, a former Miss America and
New York City Commissioner of Consumer Affairs,
expressed the rule in its most elementary form when
writing in her diary about her second husband—
"I think of him less as a man and more as a
thing that must be manipulated." Once you have
the principle firmly in hand, you can apply it to
first wives, trusted associates, aging relatives.

FAT PEOPLE

---

*A*pproach them warily. Their weight is proof
of their unhappiness, and if you spend too much time
in their company, they will lead you into debt or
psychoanalysis. The U. S. Army never promotes an
overweight officer to the rank of general.

AT THE BRIEFING

----

*T*rust to the credulity of your audience. The guests at court tend to believe that they already know everything worth knowing (otherwise how could they be guests at court?), and usually they also assume that because they know all the important people in the world, anybody whom they don't know is, by definition, unimportant. The giddy atmospheres of *amour propre* allow for very wide margins of error.

If you speak in a firm and confident voice, you can count on everybody in the room nodding in agreement at the mention of such terms as "Third Way," "Project 2000," "Laffer Curve," "Arc of Crisis," "the Andaman Domino." They won't know what the words mean, but court protocol forbids them to admit their ignorance.

For an understanding of the steady state of golden myopia, the novice careerist might want to refer to a letter sent some years ago to *The New Republic* by Morton Janklow, a New York literary agent, complaining about an article that he found disgraceful. Jacob Weisberg, the author of the article in question, had said something unpleasant (true, but unpleasant) about the New York book trade, and Janklow rebuked him for his impertinence. "I have no idea who Mr. Weisberg is, but his is not a name that I or any of my colleagues have come across in our many years of involvement with the publishing industry." Notice that the sphere of judgment coincides with the sphere of Janklow's acquaintance. Because Janklow doesn't know the scoundrel Weisberg, the scoundrel Weisberg cannot be said to exist, and his opinion is therefore worthless.

The attitude is commonplace within the councils of the great, and you should look upon it as the way to happiness and the door to fortune.

LIES

———————

*A*lways more welcome than the truth. The word is ugly, but the service never fails to please. People blessed with extraordinary talent can remember which lies they've told to which persons in what sequence and for what reasons; the beginning student should not attempt to deceive the same individual more than twice in the same afternoon. With steady practice the duplicitous response becomes as natural as a good golf swing.

L A U G H T E R

---

*T*he best people regard it as a form of verbal harassment. Bear in mind Lord Chesterfield's advice to his son: "A gentleman is only seen to smile, never heard to laugh." If you must laugh, try for a sound that can be confused with a chronic cough or a winter cold.

GRAVITAS

---

*C*areers rise on the appearance of gravity, sink
with shows of levity. Remember at all times that you
bear the burden of inside information, which is very
heavy and not to be thrown around like confetti.
When sitting at a conference table, think of
yourself as a speech by Alan Greenspan
or a trunk by Louis Vuitton.

Notes of Congratulation

———————

        *S*earch the newspapers for the names of people who have won prizes, received prestigious sums of money, been appointed to important posts. Send at least four congratulatory notes every morning before noon, taking care to match the tone of your praise with the degree of your acquaintance.

If you actually happen to know the individual, your remarks can be familiar and brief; persons with whom you enjoy only a passing acquaintance deserve two paragraphs and three tasteful adjectives; truly famous people, those whom you admire from afar, receive four paragraphs, six fulsome adjectives, and one compliment worked up into an extended metaphor that employs a reference to baseball.

Follow the same procedures when writing notes of condolence.

POLITICAL CORRECTNESS

---

*D*on't quarrel with it.

The polite forms of eighteenth-century etiquette

required your forebears to drink toasts

to the health of King George III.

THE TRAP OF
FRIENDSHIP

---

*D*o not burden yourself with the luggage of false
sentiment, and bear firmly in mind the distinction
between a connection and a friend. A connection is
an asset and a temporary convenience, like a
rented car. A friend is a liability and a
permanent obligation, like alimony.
When discussing a friendship with a fellow careerist,
refer to it as the mud that clogs the carriage
wheels of high ambition.

THE EARTHLY PARADISE

---

*I*t is a mistake to want too much, and the amateur careerist intent upon seizing everything in sight—more applause, more time with Jay Leno, more raspberry sorbet—runs the risk of falling into the state of paralysis that often incapacitated the French novelist Gustave Flaubert. Flaubert never could entirely escape the dream of infinite luxury, and sometimes he would sit for hours staring at a rosebush or a wall, imagining himself possessed of an immense fortune with which to buy English coach horses, servants taught to ease his feet into diamond-studded shoes, a dining room decorated with espaliers of flowering jasmine and the fluttering of bright-colored birds. Maxime Du Camp thought the effect comparable to an opium dream, and in his diary he remarked on it as one of the reasons that Flaubert "found steady work difficult."

As a hedge against the prospect of sitting for long hours in the lobby of the Four Seasons hotel staring at the golf bags and the plants, the professional careerist divides the sum of boundless desire into manageable fractions. Different careerists tell over to themselves different lists of available reward, but the one suggested to the White House by the Democratic National Committee during the 1996 presidential campaign comes close to describing the American garden of Eden:

1. Two reserved seats on Air Force I and II trips
2. Six seats at all White House private dinners
3. Six to eight spots at all White House events (i.e., Jazz Fest, Rose Garden ceremonies, official visits)
4. Invitations to participate in official delegation trips abroad
5. White House mess privileges

6. White House residence visits and overnight stays

7. Guaranteed Kennedy Center tickets (at least one month in advance)

8. Six radio address spots

9. Photo opportunities with the principals

10. Two places per week at the presidential CEO lunches

11. Phone time from the vice president

12. Ten places per month at White House film showings

13. One lunch with Mack McLarty per month

14. One lunch with Ira Magaziner per month

15. One lunch with the first lady per month

16. Use of the president's box at the Warner Theater and at Wolf Trap

17. Ability to reserve time on the White House tennis courts

18. Meeting time with Vice President Gore

AFTERNOON

M O V I N G   O N

———————

*A*n air of urgent haste promotes an impression of importance, and you should strive to seem always in a hurry, just now back from Paris, already late for a meeting with Mel Gibson. You wish you had time to talk, but the car is waiting, and so is the Israeli ambassador.

Apply the same strategy to the trajectory of a career. Money attaches itself to velocity. Never stay in one job for more than five years, and remember that the most important person at the party is the first one to leave the room. None of the best people travel with luggage or convictions.

IMAGE MANAGEMENT

A genuine American success requires the transformation of subject into object, flesh into brand name, self into fragrance bottle. Most people achieve the metamorphosis only in death, when they become a house in East Hampton, or a set of antique silver. The well-managed image reverses the procedure, breathing the gift of life into German automobiles, Japanese cameras, cans of Colorado beer.

It helps to think of oneself as a polo shirt. With what other merchandise would you choose to be displayed? In which stores, and how far from the shoe department? When appearing in fashion photographs, does the shirt go to the beach with Gwyneth Paltrow or to Paris with Michael Jordan? Is it blue, or is it gray? Give some thought to the questions, and you will know when to take off your hat or your dress.

OPINIONS

*T*hey must be welcome and safe. What is wanted is not so much an idea but the decent appearance of an idea, a word or a phrase sufficient to sustain an impression of consciousness.

Usually it is good to say something about the environment (as delicate as a hummingbird's wing), about the media (profoundly misinformed), about politics in Washington (irredeemably corrupt), about baseball (a more democratic game than polo). When talking about art, remember that it is a form of interior decoration; when talking about money, that it is sacred. If the host expresses a liking for carrots, mention Peter Rabbit and gardens in Connecticut.

CAMPAIGN FINANCE

Don't accept wire transfers directly from
banks in Germany or the Cayman Islands.
The money must first be sent to an American bank
and there outfitted with a new checking account,
a new name, and a hat from L. L. Bean.
The finance chairman then can walk it across
K Street to meet the vice president.

A PPETITE

———————

*H*unger implies need, which is disgraceful. When ordering lunch in the company of important people at an expensive restaurant, compose a work of minimalist art—one blackberry, one egg, one small bottle of mineral water, a single piece of dry toast.

CHARITABLE CAUSES

*A*void charities bent on improving the schools or the slums, and devote yourself instead to those that protect squirrels or flamingos. You meet a better class of people, you travel to nicer places, and you receive a better-looking baseball cap.

At the Conference

*F*it the tone of your presentation to the comfort of the accommodations. If the sponsors have gone to considerable trouble and expense (handsome views of the mountains or the sea, a first-class dining experience, aerobics classes, monogrammed golf balls, horseback riding), you can safely endorse the fierce statement of uncompromising principle and urge the call to revolution. The luxury of the setting already has decided the issue in favor of the status quo, and your opinion will be understood as decorative.

If on the other hand you find yourself in second-class surroundings (not enough towels, views of a parking lot, no chocolate on the pillow), your words might be expected to mean something. They should be mumbled and opaque, open to at least five apologies and four interpretations.

At conferences that offer a choice between the tennis and the rafting trip, choose the rafting trip. Drifting downstream encourages a pleasant state of passivity and eliminates the risk of an impolitic aggression.

RESPONSIBILITY

---

*I*t is bad for the complexion and must never be taken in large quantities. Smile graciously and pass it gently to your left—to the head of the studio, the Republican committee chairman, a Japanese bank.

Remember that as an American you inherit the gift of innocence by right of birth. Foreigners incite wars, manufacture cocaine, sponsor terrorists, and breed disease; Americans cleanse the world of its impurities. Foreigners commit crimes against humanity; Americans make well-intentioned mistakes.

CHILDREN AND DOGS

---

*B*efriend them. Their good opinion speaks to your character as a person deserving of confidence and trust. When invited for a weekend in the country, remember to bring a rubber ball. Bounce it for the child; throw it for the dog.

HYPOCRISY

---

*Y*our most faithful ally
and truest friend.
You cannot afford to leave home
without it.

CASH

$\mathcal{D}$on't go to an important meeting or golf game without at least $500 in your wallet or your purse. The presence of the cash instills an attitude of calm. Even a modest sum of money stands surrogate for all the pleasurable states of feeling into which it can be transferred, and its reassuring weight serves as a prescription against panic. Some people think of it as a way of holding their mother's hand.

———————

A good author is a rich author, and a rich author is a good author. The demonstrated capacity to make money confers the certificate of genius.

Any book that you keep on a shelf for longer than four months you may presume to have read. The aging process makes the author's name familiar enough to drop with confidence into a conversation about capitalism or the Balkans. If you happen to see the author on a television talk show, or if you encounter his or her name in a gossip column, you may claim knowledge of the book after only two months.

THE DISTINCTION
BETWEEN A
WINSOME BLURB AND AN
ANGRY REVIEW

A winsome blurb is a tribute to the courage of the human spirit; an angry review is an insult to the goodness of your fellowman. Always write the winsome blurb; never write the angry review.

The rule sometimes can be overlooked when discussing the work of a foreign or unknown writer, but if an editor asks you for 1,000 words of "honest criticism" of a new book by a much-praised author, flee from the request as if from a Muslim with a bomb. The defenders of settled opinion have spent twenty years inflating the currency of the author's reputation, and an angry review constitutes an attack not only upon a beloved persona, but also and more important, on a substantial investment. The attack on the author could be forgiven; the attack on money is blasphemy.

GRANT PROPOSALS

---

*T*he language of the successful grant proposal achieves the pallor of the color beige. Avoid concrete nouns and vivid adjectives, and remember to employ the word "enhance." You are not seeking money for reasons of your own self-aggrandizement. Certainly not. The thought is monstrous. You wish to enhance and enrich the public understanding—of our beloved democratic heritage or the situation in Albania. Never write a proposal in the first person singular. The correct voice is the voice of a committee.

CAMERAS

----

*W*hen confronted by a photographer with a
still camera, you may strike a flamboyant or
expressive pose. The fanciful attitude will appear as
the whim of a moment, and you will be forgiven for it.
The television camera doesn't extend the same
courtesy. Any interview that continues for longer than
three minutes imprisons the subject within an image
that might take twenty years to correct or escape.
The well-behaved guest should strive for the polite
quietness of highly polished wood. No fidgeting,
no drumming of fingers on the studio table,
no unrehearsed jokes.

BLAME

---

*A*ssign it to acronyms, random accident,
historical forces, or people too weak to do you any
harm. Don't mention the names of specific
individuals. One or more of them might
be standing in the room.
When arriving late for an appointment, it is the fault
of the traffic or the rain; when filing for divorce, it is
the fault of postmodernism. Rock music lost the war
in Vietnam; soft-headed liberalism wrecked the public
schools; television poisoned the wells of conscience
and dimmed the lamps of civility.

HONORIFICS

*I*f two Americans otherwise unknown to each other meet on an airplane or a golf course, the answer to the question, "Who are you with?" determines which one owes the other what measures of notice and respect. The institutional identity—Mobil Oil, J. P. Morgan, *The New York Times*, Microsoft—corresponds to the honorific "de" attached to the names of the French nobility in seventeenth- and eighteenth-century France. Women escape the formality of having to wear a title to East Hampton or the opera, but not the man who wishes to advance the flag of his ambition.

The lesson impressed itself upon me in August of 1981, when I was dismissed as the editor of *Harper's*

Magazine and so remanded to oblivion. The telephone stopped ringing as abruptly as if the wires had been cut by terrorists, but a few days before the news of my departure appeared in the papers, I had accepted an invitation to a September dinner at the Council on Foreign Relations in honor of Giscard d'Estaing, then the recently retired president of France. The social secretary issuing the invitation explained that the guest list would be very short, restricted to only those few people in New York deemed capable of appreciating d'Estaing's subtlety and wit.

Four days before the dinner she called to confirm my attendance, but by that time, of course, I was no longer the editor of *Harper's Magazine*, and my lack of a suitable title caused her a good deal of embarrassment and alarm. After what seemed like a very long silence, she said that she didn't know how she could proceed unless I could align my name with that of an important organization. She was terribly sorry, and she wished that she didn't have to remind me that it was the council's practice to distribute the guest list to all those present at the table, but what, after all, could she do? Never in the years of her service had anybody ever come to dinner without the dignity of an institutional connection.

She was genuinely upset, and in an effort to relieve her of her anxiety, I said that I occasionally wrote a column for the op-ed page of *The Washington Post*. It wasn't a syndicated column, and it appeared so infrequently that it was scarcely noticeable, but at least it had a more or less regular place on the page. The woman's relief was as heartfelt as it was audible. Oh, she said, I was sure that we could think of something, and I know that President d'Estaing will be pleased. I told her how much I admired the president, and how much I looked forward to hearing what he had to say about the fate of nations and the destiny of mankind.

The dinner was even smaller than expected—a single table of twelve instead of the usual four or five tables of eight—and I found myself placed next to Katherine Graham, the owner and publisher of *The Washington Post*. It was quite clear that she didn't know that I wrote for her paper. It was equally clear that she never had heard my name mentioned in what she considered an important conversation. Her silence was sufficiently expressive to convey her suspicion that I was either a rank impostor or somebody who composed the classifieds for men seeking women and women seeking men. When at last it was permissible to leave, I remember Mrs. Graham looking at me as if she were sure that as soon as I stepped into the street I would be met with a warrant for my arrest.

THE MASK OF IRONY

*T*he correct expression is slightly
contemptuous and faintly amused.
Admire everything and nothing. Never show surprise.
Do not gawk. Remember that you have seen
everything worth seeing, not once but many, many
times before. The attitude defers judgment—also
commitment and possible mistakes—and when
displayed in the form of writing or speech,
it serves as a substitute for dissent.

DISSENT

---

*N*ot a good career move. You forfeit the confidence of your patrons and business associates, and you don't make any new friends. Nobody welcomes contradiction, and you will come to be known as a malcontent, a spoilsport, not a team player, a sore thumb.

Free speech extended beyond the bounds of good taste is an indulgence, like problem drinking. If you can't rid yourself of the habit, find an obscure coffee shop or motel bar in which, once or twice a month, you may astonish the company with the courage of your own unmediated opinions. Back in the office or the newsroom, suggest modifications, recommend improvements and amendments, congratulate your superiors for the breadth of their good intentions, their perspicacity, the boldness of their vision.

Of all the great American sermons the greatest is the one about "staying viable within the system," and although I've heard it preached for forty years by adepts as deft as President Clinton and Oliver North, never have I heard it more perfectly expressed than by Dan Rather, before and after his journey to China in 1972 with President Nixon's press entourage.

A week before the plane left for Beijing, Rather showed up in the offices of *Harper's Magazine* with his ghostwriter, and together they told a melodramatic story of a president wandering, like King Lear, on the near shores of madness—the White House captured by treacherous sycophants, Nixon raving, democratic government drifting into anarchy, vile plots and secret CIA money.

All of which Rather volunteered to disclose in print. Strong stuff, he said, and not apt to boost his ratings west of the Hudson River, but how could he do otherwise? He had the facts and served the truth. But first he must go to China, there to more closely observe the corruption of the president and the president's men. He would return, he said, even more heavily armed with the weight of evidence.

We set a deadline, agreed to a price and measure of words, and Rather grasped my hand with the fervor of a bomber pilot leaving for a combat mission in a movie about the last days of Nazi Germany. I never found out what he knew or didn't know. Nixon's journey to China preceded by two months the confusion at the Watergate, and it's conceivable that Rather had come across some early news of conspiracy and criminal intent. If so, he decided that the American people were better served by his continued presence in the White House (i.e., "staying viable within the system") than by his reckless speaking out of turn.

Or so at least he said, when, two weeks after his return from China, he presented an explanation in lieu of a manuscript.

"Outside the White House," he said, "I'm no good to anybody. Inside the White House I defend the cause of liberty."

No patriot ever spoke more boldly.

AT THE TELEVISION INTERVIEW

The correct attitude is grateful and abject. The
ladies and gentlemen of the fourth estate open and
close the doors to the lighted rooms of celebrity,
and they must never—repeat, never—
be made to look foolish.
When talking to Ted Koppel, the wise careerist
imagines himself speaking to the late Charles de
Gaulle or to one of the stones on Easter Island.
In the presence of Geraldo Rivera the attribution of
gravitas is more difficult, but the awkwardness can
be overcome by thinking of Geraldo as a Renaissance
prince in a portrait by Bronzino, his fatuousness
redeemed by the dignity of an ermine cloak and
the lilt of a velvet hat.

PRIZE COMMITTEES

―――――――――

*W*hen serving on prize committees, remember that the agenda doesn't refer to last year's film, last year's book, last year's hope for world peace. What you are talking about is the awarding of next year's prizes, when your own work becomes eligible for a ribbon or a statuette. You are making connections, not judgments, which is why it is best to give the prize to the mediocre, the second-rate, the politically correct—i.e., to weakness unlikely to threaten your own reputation or book-club sales.

WHEN BORROWING MONEY

---

*L*oan officers look upon borrowers as pilgrims
come to make confession, and they can smell
desperation or need in the same way that animals can
smell fear. Even if you stand in imminent peril of
losing wife, child, house, and reputation, affect an
attitude of mild indifference; require $1 million
instead of $100,000, and imagine that you
are speaking to your tailor.

STATESMANSHIP

---

*P*rofit from your reading of otherwise dull
articles on the subject of foreign policy by recognizing
the phrase "national interest" as a synonym for
"self-interest." Apply the same set of recommended
actions to your own affairs, and you will find no crime
that cannot be justified, no friend who cannot be
de-accessioned, no debt that cannot be repudiated,
no moral obstacle that cannot be removed from the
highway of ambition.

P O S S E S S I O N S

---

*P*ossessions testify not only to social status but also to an individual's worth as a human being. Small and shabby collections belong to small and shabby souls. Act accordingly.

Among the nouveau riche you may compare possessions in the way that children match birthday presents or trade baseball cards; mention the exact length of the motor boat, the engine capacity of the sports car, the name of the famous author who writes your host's after-dinner speeches.

The older money prefers to compare memories. Remark on the quality of your great-grandmother's iced tea, the paintings in the hall at Newport, the way the lawn looked that summer of Didi's dance.

INSOLENCE

---

*T*he Ivy League universities teach the attitude as a matter of course, which is why the tuitions sell for $28,000 a year, but students matriculating at less prestigious colleges can learn it by watching *Late Night with David Letterman* and listening carefully to the voices of the celebrity guests. Notice that the jokes turn on the theme of wealth surprised by poverty—the rich man amazed by the dinginess of third-tier orange juice, astonished by the discomfort of low-grade motels, disappointed in the seating plan on a Greyhound bus. The guests present themselves as art objects temporarily on loan from Mount Olympus or Palm Springs.

Further instances of the proper tone decorate the pages of *The New Yorker* and *Vanity Fair*, and beginning students can practice its finer expressions as if they were playing musical scales:

Leona Helmsley—"Taxes are for the little people."

Jackie Stewart—"My dogs have never flown commercial."

Chevy Chase—"Malibu smells like anchovies."

WHEN IN CALIFORNIA

*M*ore often than not the person to whom one happens to be speaking turns out to be playing a part in his or her own movie. If a man identifies himself as a writer, it might mean that he writes notes to his dog, in green ink on a special kind of yellow paper that he buys in Paris; if a woman says that she's an actress, it might mean that she once stood next to Kevin Costner in an airport and that he looked at her in such a way that she knew he thought she was under contract to Universal.

Accept the statements at face value. Compliment the writer on his resemblance to the young Charles Dickens; encourage the actress to discuss the work of Orson Welles.

DEMOCRACY

---

*N*ot a subject that you're likely to know much about. Leave the discussion of its finer points to Harvard professors and New York City cabdrivers.

BOREDOM

---

*D*utiful attendance at the knee of privilege presupposes the capacity to endure long bouts of stupefying boredom. Because the topics of conversation never change, it is by no means easy to stay awake, much less remember when to utter sudden exclamations of delight and surprise.

Practice with inanimate objects. Look at a balloon for ninety minutes with an expression of close attention and profound respect; talk to a box of Cheerios about Martha's Vineyard and Monica Lewinsky; ask a fern for its view of the Mexican debt. The exercises will prepare you for an evening at the Council of Foreign Relations or an afternoon around the pool with Norman Mailer.

AT THE
WHITE HOUSE

---

*N*ever give or take money on government property. At the coffee ceremony in the Map Room of the White House, praise the coffee, eat no more than one Danish pastry, remark that the Map Room must have been a swell and exciting place in President Roosevelt's time (because he was using the maps to chart the course of World War II), praise the president on any pretext that comes to mind (for his sympathy toward poor people or the steadiness of his golf swing), sip the coffee, compliment all the other people in the room (for their youth and vigor, never for their clothes or their jewels), inquire about the chance of rain, rise gracefully when a bell rings and the president is called away, praise the usher in the Marine uniform (not the steward in the white coat), walk proudly out of the building along the line of march indicated by the doorkeepers, praise the coffee once again (to anybody still within earshot), and so regain the anonymity of a common thoroughfare or public street. Then and only then is it permissible to write the check, which can be handed (in an envelope either blank or engraved) to a nearby aide-de-camp, who will carry it gingerly around the perimeter of the White House (being very, very careful not to step on the driveway or the lawn) to an office of the Democratic National Committee, where women in flowered dresses spray it with eau de cologne.

Similar protocols must be observed when purchasing lesser politicians, but circumstances vary, and the formalities occasionally can be abbreviated. If you find yourself riding in a car with a senator from Utah or a congressman from Texas, and if you wish to express your appreciation for his or her selfless and devoted service to the American people, and unless you happen to be driving through a military base or an Indian reservation, it is permissible to hand the check to the senator's assistant, even to stuff it into the assistant's pocket with a hearty laugh or a friendly nudge.

CHANGING SIDES

---

*T*he best people in New York and Los Angeles change their moral certainties as often as they change their sheets, and you can learn the art by studying department-store show windows. Just as different seasons require different costumes, so also the several stages of a career require different attitudes, different friends, different unshakable beliefs.

When dressing for an afternoon stroll to the winning side, you might wish to remember that idealism is a spring color that goes well with Bermuda shorts and cotton tank tops; treachery is an autumn tone, appropriate in both wool and cashmere.

Once arrived in new company, you should strive for a facial expression that is frank, open, and ingenuous. Think of yourself as the prodigal son who has come safely home. At long last and after much foolishness, you have seen a great light, which, with good image management and a decent run of luck, will see you through the winter in Aspen.

EVENING

ON BEING SEEN

In sixteenth-century London and seventeenth-century France, ambition made its way upward in the world by being seen at court. The genius of modern technology substitutes the settings of the television studio, the gossip column, and the fashion magazine for the palaces at Greenwich and Versailles. Seize every photo opportunity; accept every invitation to an interview. Fortify yourself every morning with Gore Vidal's first, last, and only word of advice to a young writer—"Never miss a chance to have sex or appear on television."

A truly fashionable dinner party ends at the moment when all the guests have arrived and everybody has been seen or not seen. If the other people present are richer or more famous than oneself, the value of one's name and reputation can be said to be rising; if the other people are poorer or less famous, it is time to buy another baseball team.

Once attendance has been taken, the rest of the evening is superfluous. The guests might as well be made of Venetian glass and filled with lemon mousse.

INVITATIONS

---

*N*ever accept an invitation without first discovering who else has been asked to the party. You don't need to know the name of everybody on the list, but you must know what class of guest the host or sponsor has in mind—A-list people or B-list people, principal or supporting cast, next year's probable presidential candidate or last year's Miss Honolulu.

Assuming that you recognize three or more important names, and if somebody other than a press agent confirms the certain arrival of those names (as opposed to the amiable possibility of their maybe stopping by) you may leak the news of your own attendance to Cindy Adams.

FLATTERY

---

*C*omparable to suntan lotion or moisturizing cream, also to furniture polish and ski wax. It cannot be too often or too recklessly applied.

The novice careerist might think that very important people grow tired of hearing themselves praised, that they will find the intention too obvious and therefore insincere. The presumption is false. Important people hear little else except praise, and they tend to regard all other forms of speech as un-American.

But even the happiest repetitions pall, and the sweetest flatteries turn stale unless refreshed by new and joyous discoveries of unsuspected virtue and talents previously unknown. Vary the adjectives and angles of approach. Remark on the beauty of the chairman's stamp collection, the subtlety of the in-genue's understanding of Weimar Germany; praise the bond trader for the shape of her foot, the statesman for his playing of the banjo.

At the decisive pause in the conversation never miss a cue for the mandatory compliment, no matter how hackneyed or trite. Hesitation implies doubt, which is insulting. The lizard eye of greatness closes as silently and abruptly as the lights going down on a failed play.

MORAL SCRUPLES

―――――――――――

*T*hey can be safely exposed when giving
a commencement speech or speaking to
a television camera, but they become dangerous
when left lying carelessly around in
one's own office or bedroom, in a suit pocket
or on a beach towel.

THE GUEST LIST

A memorable dinner party numbers among the guests at least one individual suspected of an important crime, preferably murder. The presence of a tabloid criminal darkens the room with an atmosphere of intimate sadism, an effect that the best New York hostesses liken to candlelight.

During the few months before he was shot to death in Umberto's Clam House, Joey Gallo, a well-known Mafia figure and *bon vivant*, enjoyed a brief vogue in Manhattan as a fun sort of person to have around. He occasionally appeared at Elaine's, a restaurant frequented by media celebrities, and his arrival inevitably caused the talk in the room to abruptly die away into the stillness that constituted the establishment's highest mark of esteem.

Failing an acquaintance with O. J. Simpson or Claus von Bulow, you can generate something of the same excitement with a corrupt police detective, a notorious madam, or Dennis Rodman.

WORKING THE ROOM

*D*on't go to the room; let the room come to you.
Too much moving around implies anxiety and need,
which in turn suggests an unhappy comparison to
Mortimer Zuckerman or an undernourished ferret.
Stand quietly somewhere between the foyer and the
buffet table, and try for an appearance as
obliging as the toasted cheese.

TOPICS OF
CONVERSATION

*G*uests invited to small dinners for President Reagan received a telephone call on the afternoon prior to the event in which it was explained by one of Reagan's social advisors that the president preferred the conversation "light," safely confined to sports, gossip, and movies. President Bush substituted geography for movies, and President Clinton substitutes policy analysis for all movies except *Saving Private Ryan*, but otherwise the list of topics remains constant.

The mention of money in large enough denominations never fails to command respect. If you wish to attract the attention of the company at a cocktail or dinner party, usually it is sufficient to speak of your recent encounter with a sum in excess of $500 million.

Maybe you have just had lunch with somebody who sold Atlantic City to the Deutsche Bank; perhaps you have fresh news of an expensive divorce or a merger of telephone companies said to amount to $34 billion. You need not know any of the individuals privy to the deal. The money achieves the stature of celebrity, almost as if it were Tiger Woods or Cameron Diaz, and your audience, whether of corporation presidents or university professors allegedly Marxist, will admire you for your sense of propriety, your good taste, your dedication to America's family values, your choice of friends.

THE BEST PEOPLE

---

*Y*ou recognize them by their clothes,
not their character.

THE SERVILE SMILE

$\mathcal{T}$he smile must be flexible yet firm, conveying principled approval as well as eager assent. Think of a waiter in a Las Vegas restaurant bringing Bruce Willis a lobster or a blonde, or Diane Sawyer interviewing a celebrity whose net worth exceeds $40 million. Of course you wish to do your patron's bidding (who in his right mind would not?), but, more important, you understand the brilliance of the word, the rightness of the act. The lips should be slightly parted, the head tilted expectantly upward, the expression one of barely suppressed amazement.

The smile shows to its best effect when accompanied by small exclamations of spontaneous joy—"How beautiful!" "How wise!"

GOSSIP

----

*D*on't make the mistake of thinking gossip trivial or unimportant. The telling of a lurid anecdote about the corporate chairman's shoe fetish or the movie star's arrest marks you as a person of consequence, somebody who enjoys a wide acquaintance among the company of the great.

Do not dwell on the details. You wish to convey an air of knowingness, not a proof of knowledge, and by attempting too elaborate a narrative, you run the risk of getting it wrong. Somebody else in the room (the movie star's lawyer, the corporate chairman's mistress) might have better information, and you will be seen as a mere reader of cheap newspapers.

S L A N D E R

---

*T*he best and most satisfactory form of gossip,
especially when smeared on the names of people who
happen to be rich, good-looking, or famous. If even
Harrison Ford or Nicole Kidman can be made to look
as stupid as oneself, one's own mediocrity and
resentment become easier to bear.

When invited to spend a weekend with important
journalists or movie stars in Sag Harbor, it is
considered polite to bring three or four malicious
libels in lieu of a house gift or a bottle of wine.

SERVANTS

———————

*A*ddress them respectfully, as if they were fellow-members of the Cosmos Club or friends of Donald Trump; they represent the democratic hopes of oppressed populations seeking to escape the miseries of the Third World.

Once you have learned to ask pleasantly about the health of the cook's husband, you will know how to talk to Wesley Snipes about the Civil War, what to say to *Time* magazine about Susan B. Anthony.

APPLAUSE

$\mathcal{E}$stimate the cost of the production, remembering to add the market price of the celebrities in the cast, and clap accordingly. A Broadway play starring Leonardo de Caprio is a better play than one starring Meryl Streep. The same rule obtains at fund-raising dinners. The philanthropist who announces a $500,000 gift to Israel or multiple sclerosis deserves a louder and longer volley of applause than the philanthropist who gives $250,000. On the announcement of sums in excess of $1 million it is customary to rise to one's feet.

When in doubt, look to see who else is applauding and match your enthusiasm to the degree of approval expressed by those celebrities in the audience whom you have seen on the cover of *Vanity Fair*.

WIT

---

*N*early always ill-advised. Women fear and detest it. The well-turned phrase balances on too keen an edge or too sharp a point. Learn from the example of the Washington press corps, which makes its annual attempt at humor at the banquet presented by the Gridiron Club. The club holds fast to its motto "Singe but never burn," and hires professional comedians to write the harmless jokes.

But even harmless jokes always must be introduced with warnings like those printed on cigarette packages. Never tell one without first informing the company of your intent. If you forget to explain that you heard the joke from somebody else, on television, or the

commuter train, it will be said that you lack serious-
ness, and you will be reduced to the rank of the paid
entertainment.

UNDERSTATEMENT

---

*Y*es, you have spent a night in the Lincoln Bedroom, but you don't make a story of the experience. If somebody else at the table describes his or her evening in the same room, don't interrupt. Let the anecdote run its course, and then, at the end, ask if the staff had gotten around to washing the windows or fixing the lamp.

RIDICULE

----

*F*ear it.

A GOOD BUTLER

When dining in households that employ the service of a good butler, study the man's conduct and deportment. Learn to imitate his expression as well as his movements, and you'll understand what the politicians mean by the word "consensus." You also will have taken a first step toward a career as a television anchorperson.

In the Presence of the Check

The proper moment for an inspirational anecdote or a funny story. Saying good-bye to money is never easy, and the awful silence that descends on the table when the waiter brings the check is like the silence that accompanies the news of a death in the family. Express your sympathy by diverting the host's attention to the memory of a successful golf score or the life of a long-suffering saint.

DROPPING NAMES

----

*C*ollect both the private and public names of
prominent celebrities. Like jade bracelets or
medicinal herbs, they protect you against the scorn
of headwaiters, the insolence of hotel clerks,
the mockery of pool attendants.
Among people of superior status, drop only the
private name—"Brad," "Babs," "George." Among
persons of inferior status, drop both names—
Brad Pitt, Barbara Walters, George Soros.
In the first instance you are presenting letters of
recommendation; in the second,
throwing coins to beggars.

THROWING FOOD

---

*T*he diversion is popular with some of the younger heirs to Protestant fortunes, possibly because it eliminates the tiresome business of taking an interest in, much less contributing to, the conversation. Don't throw at the hostess unless she throws at you first. The bread, not the salad or the stew; never at the Armani.

GALAS, BENEFITS, CHARITY BALLS

---

*T*hey exist to be photographed. Nobody expects you to say anything important; nor does it matter whether the conversation is as boring as the food, whether the other guests in attendance have nothing in common except the ability to pay $10,000 for a table and $30,000 for a dress. Follow the photographers and try to stand next to the most important person in the room. What matters is your name on the list and your face in the next day's news.

Momentous social occasions often divide into two parts, the larger and more public event followed by a private dinner or reception. Don't attend the former unless you also have been invited to the latter. At the moment of decision, when the prettier people are getting into cars and asking each other the way to Mary's pool or Harry's bar, you will be seen to have been cast as a lawn jockey, of no more consequence than the shrimp. Avoid the indignity by declining the first invitation. Say that you would have loved to come if only you weren't in Spain that week with Clint Eastwood.

Invitations to historic events—those social occasions to which *People* allots more than six pages of photographs—acquire the significance of state documents. They should be framed in silver and displayed on a mantelpiece with the photographs of oneself at Malibu in the rain.

SEXUAL FERVOR

*C*orrectly enjoyed in the presence of ob-jects, not in the company of human beings. Even Bill Clinton once understood the point. While campaigning for his first presidential term in the autumn of 1992, he was asked by a *New York Times* reporter to list the re-quirements for a successful political career. He pro-posed six rules, the second of which touched upon the question of abstinence:

"When you're starting to have a good time," he said, "you're supposed to be somewhere else."

You cannot make a mistake if you think of sexual fantasy as a kind of lip gloss meant to improve the sale of office equipment and Caribbean cruises. Remember to look, not touch, to give way to your passions in a department store or automobile showroom, never in a cocktail lounge.

SELF-PITY

All the best people feel sorry for themselves.
It is how one knows that they are the best people.
Their admissions of fear and weakness demonstrate
their refinement of feeling.
Comfort them with stories about how the world has
failed them, why nothing works anymore, and where
have all the servants gone? If you strike the
appropriately disappointed tone, you can direct the
same set of remarks to a gray hair, the collapse of
the Democratic party, or a dead bulldog.

ADULTERY

---

*A*lthough in some social circles in Los Angeles and New York it is still considered polite to seduce the person next to whom one finds oneself seated at dinner, the courtesy need not be as strictly observed as it was during the heyday of the Kennedy administration. The sexual harassment laws have blown out the candles of romance.

Exchange business cards instead of ardent glances, postponing the appointment until two weeks from next Monday, when both your calendars show an unscheduled afternoon in Indianapolis or Orlando. Do not bolt from the table in a gust of sudden passion. Try not to look like President Clinton posing for photographs with a new golf ball.

WHEN IN WASHINGTON

*A*t Washington dinner parties it is only the parvenu rustics from Los Angeles and New York who discuss the front-page news about health insurance or the trouble in Afghanistan. The cognoscenti talk about Congressman Dan Burton hunting pumpkins, where Monica Lewinsky buys her lipstick, or Dick Morris transformed into a newspaper sage by virtue of his long and diligent study of a call girl's toes.

The tone of voice never varies, no matter who happens to occupy the White House or what the season's flow of news. Through the spring and summer of 1991, in the midst of the dissolution of the Soviet Union and the end of forty years of American geopolitical theory, Ted Koppel and the hostesses on P Street were preoccupied with the far greater questions of John Sununu's passion for government limousines and Teddy Kennedy's cameo appearances in the fleshpots of Palm Beach. Was it true that in New Hampshire Sununu was sometimes carried through the streets in an eighteenth-century sedan chair? Could anybody imagine any of the Kennedys ever growing up?

On the answers to such questions depend one's hope of appointment to the Federal Trade Commission or an invitation to sit with Cokie and Sam around the campfire at ABC News.

VICE

———————

More profitably studied than virtue.
Virtue commands respect, which is a liability;
also admiration, which is not amusing.
The people apt to do you the most good presumably
possess the kind of money that expects a good time.
Fall in with their whims, pander to their lusts,
approve their injustices, admire their deformities
and their furniture. They hold in their hands
the answers to all your prayers.

CIGARETTE SMOKING

---

*I*f you find yourself seated with important movie
people in a Beverly Hills restaurant, and if you
happen to see someone smoking at the bar, you may
walk up to that person and slap the cigarette out of
his or her hand. The important movie people will
appreciate the gesture as an expression of concern for
their safety. The more sensitive among them might
write you an option on a napkin.

ANDROGYNY

---

*L*earn to stage both a masculine and feminine performance of your character. Gender is a liquid asset, like cash or Treasury bills, and under proper management it can be made to flow into whatever shape serves the interest of the money in the room. Stand-up comics and political consultants make the best instructors, but you also may apply for advice to the nearest journalist. For an indication of the proper stance and look, study those fashion advertisements in which both the boys and girls appear to be dressed as parachutists.

MAKING CONFESSIONS

*I*t doesn't matter whether you do so in public or in private as long as you remember to limit the admission to a general tendency—drunkenness, dishonesty, self-loathing, homophobia—and avoid mentioning particular incidents, specific names, exact dates. Yes, you've been known to gamble, and once upon a time in the 1960s you were in a room where people were smoking marijuana; no, you don't know Cindy Lou Metcalf, and you've never heard of anybody named Maurice.

TACT

A career succeeds or fails not so much by reason of what one does or neglects to do as by one's refusal to give or take offense. The deft careerist learns to swallow insults as if they were oysters served on silver trays.

When pressed for illustration of the desired habit of mind, I think of Warren Hoge at the Metropolitan Museum in the spring of 1984, standing at attention with a towel over his arm, smiling at a palm tree in the Temple of Dendur, clutching a bottle of champagne. On the evening in question Hoge was the editor of *The New York Times Magazine*, in which had appeared that same day and at Hoge's direction a caustic article about the Prince and Princess of Wales, married for no more than a few months and on their way to Washington for a royal visit. The cover art was cartoonish, the text mocking and sarcastic, the presentation an attempt at being clever.

Or so it had seemed to Hoge when he committed it to print, three weeks before he was summoned to dinner at the Egyptian temple under glass, a dinner given by Arthur Sulzberger, publisher of *The New York Times*, in honor of his great and good friend, Walter Annenberg, the ambassador to the Court of St. James. Annenberg was an admirer of all things British, and he'd never met a duke, much less a princess or a prince, in whose voice he didn't hear the sound of George Frideric Handel's *Water Music*.

Arriving among the early guests, Hoge was told that Annenberg was not amused. It was said that the ambassador thought the article tasteless and disrespectful, that he was angry (very angry), that he had been complaining all afternoon about the boor who edited *The New York Times Magazine*.

What to do? How to avoid compounding the offense? What if Annenberg in the company of Sulzberger should stumble upon Hoge's presence as if upon a toad? What then? My God, what if Sulzberger found himself obliged to introduce the ambassador to the toad?

Telling the story seven years later, Hoge remembered "the awful moment" as possibly the worst of his career—a crisis more difficult and complex than any he'd encountered as a foreign correspondent in the jungles of Brazil or Vietnam. Fortunately, he said, he was quick-witted and resourceful, as was to be expected of a journalist of rank, and he instantly recognized the parallel to Edgar Allen Poe's story "The Purloined Letter." Clearly it was a question of hiding in plain sight, at least for the duration of the reception. At the dinner, which was set up in the largest of the temple's stone courtyards, he had been assigned to a table so distant from the ambassador's dais that he might as well be sitting somewhere in Queens. But at the reception people were free to move around, which was what made the situation problematic, "dangerous, you see," Hoge said, "because subject to accident."

The simplicity of his solution he presented with the

pride of the man who had solved the magazine's cross-word puzzle. "A waiter," he said, "I changed places with a waiter. For fifty dollars I borrowed his champagne bottle and his towel, and for forty-five minutes I stood next to a statue of Osiris, as invisible as night. Like the guests that evening, the waiters were dressed in black tie, and nobody saw me because nobody looked."

THE LIMELIGHT

---

*N*ot a safe place. Approach it slowly over a long
and gradual curve of time. Too steep an ascent into
the atmospheres of fame invites a correspondingly
steep descent to the base camp of anonymity. The
intersection of the two lines form what is known as
The Warhol Salient—i.e., the fifteen minutes of fame
that immediately precede the return to oblivion.

Conscience

*N*o matter what crimes a man may have committed, or how cynically a woman may have debased her talent or her friends, variations on the answer, "Yes, but I did it for the money," satisfy all but the most tiresome objections.

The desire for wealth might not be an attractive passion, but as an explanation it answers for most modes of conduct that otherwise might be construed as stupid, cruel, or self-defeating.

As a remedy against the discomfort of doubt or guilt, fondle your stock portfolio or your jewels and consider the dilemma of the citizen who wishes to acquire a reputation for villainy. What, as a practical matter, could the fellow do? He could traffic in child pornography or indulge a taste for cannibalism. Offenses of lesser magnitude merely invite the usual offers from Home Box Office and Charlie Rose.

I N   T H E   L O O P

---

*Y*ou know that you have arrived when you see
that the pictures on the walls resemble the ones that
you remember from nursery school—ducks and
horses, mountains or the seashore, many boats.

About the Author

LEWIS LAPHAM was born in 1935 in San Francisco, California and educated at the Hotchkiss School, Yale University (BA 1956), and Cambridge University. He has been a reporter for the *San Francisco Examiner* (1957–1959) and for *The New York Herald Tribune* (1960–1962); managing editor of *Harper's Magazine* (1971–1975); editor of *Harper's Magazine* (1976–1981 and 1983–present). He was a syndicated newspaper columnist from 1981–1987. He has also written for *Life, Commentary, National Review, Elle, Fortune, Forbes, Vanity Fair, Parade, The Observer* (London), *The New York Times*, and *The Wall Street Journal*. He is the host and the author of a six-part documentary series, *America's Century*, broadcast on public television in 1989. Between 1989 and 1991, he was the host and executive editor of *Bookmark*, a weekly public television series seen on over 150 stations nationwide.

Mr. Lapham lives in New York City with his wife and three children.

ABOUT THE TYPE

This book was set in Bodoni, a typeface designed by
Giambattista Bodoni (1740–1813), the renowned Italian
printer and type designer. Bodoni originally based his
letter forms on those of the Frenchman Fournier,
and created his type to have beautiful contrasts
between light and dark.